And There Goes *My Life*

GILMA GREEN

BALBOA.
PRESS
A DIVISION OF HAY HOUSE

Balboa Press books may be ordered through booksellers or by contacting:

Balboa Press
A Division of Hay House
1663 Liberty Drive
Bloomington, IN 47403
www.balboapress.com
1 (877) 407-4847

Printed in the United States of America.

ISBN: 978-1-4525-1799-5 (sc)
ISBN: 978-1-4525-1800-8 (e)

Balboa Press rev. date: 9/12/2014

Introduction

Day in and day out, I saw young adults making horrible choices that altered their life forever. I could see that they didn't even realize what power they had to control their lives. Even at a young age, they had more power than they gave themselves credit. They could alter their destiny for good or bad. It is all determined by their attitude and their choices.

I saw so many people from good families totally wreck their future. Then to the contrary, despite terrible odds, some people overcame horrible circumstances and succeed.

Through analysis, I started to realize that the common factor to all of the stories, good or bad, was attitude and choices. I thought about writing this book for many years. If this book can help even one person realize that their choices and attitude have a huge impact on their future success or failure, then I'll consider this book a success.

It is filled with true, real life stories. Some of the stories aren't pretty, but then sometimes neither is life. It's our perseverance that will ultimately help us.

Dedication

This book is dedicated to my brother, John. Out of my five siblings, he was the one who always took the time to listen to me and play with me. He had a simple kindness that you don't find in most people. It's sad that everything can change in a New York minute. His life has taught me many lessons and has opened my eyes to how our choices can quickly change our destiny in a microsecond.

And There Goes

My Life

Table of Contents

Drugs

It all started when I was eight years old. I'm a happy kid. I am in the third grade and things are going great. I have an awesome teacher. She is exciting and wears great clothes. Things are good at home. Life is simple.

However, one day everything changes. As I get off the bus and get closer to my house, I notice that all of the tires are popped on our two cars. "How could all of the tires pop at once?" I think to myself. As I enter my house, I notice that my entire house is in total disarray. Things are thrown everywhere. There are bookshelves turned over and clothes thrown everywhere. It feels as if there isn't one inch of the floor that doesn't have something on it.

As I approach the living room, I see my brother lying on the couch, with his arms folded. I've never seen him so angry and so evil. The look in his eyes is frightening. His eyes are dark and he is extremely enraged. I hear him threaten to kill my mother. What could possibly being going on? I think to myself. This is my kind, caring brother. Why is he so different? I feel like I'm in some kind of a bad movie.

My mother, who is a moderately nervous person, is extremely calm. Instead of overreacting and making the situation worse, she calmly goes to our neighbor's house to get help. The Police come and take my brother away. He is admitted to a psychiatric hospital for observation.

I later learned the story that lead up to that dark day. My brother had been out with his friends. They were at a party and someone had brown LSD. My brother's friend took one pill of LSD and my brother took two pills. The friend later said that the LSD was extremely strong and it made him hallucinate. He couldn't believe that my brother took two pills of LSD because the one pill that he took had such a severe effect on him. He told my family that after the party, my brother became extremely paranoid. He wouldn't return his phone calls. My brother became more and more isolated and paranoid, until one day, he snapped.

He was later diagnosed as a paranoid schizophrenic. He was sent to live at McLean's Hospital in Belmont, Massachusetts. This hospital is well known for top notch psychiatric care. However, to an eight year old girl, it is an extremely scary place.

My mother took me to see him. The first thing that

I noticed is that everything is locked. They let you in a locked door and they lock the door behind you. When you want to leave they have to unlock the door for you. As I walked down the halls, I heard patients chanting all kinds of words that didn't make sense to me. The words are not coherent; they are all thrown together without making sense. It is a very unsettling feeling. When I saw my brother, he was drugged and was no longer the brother that I had known. It was very hard for me to comprehend what was going on because I was so young. All I knew is that something had changed my brother and it was very, very scary.

As the years went by, my brother was in and out of psychiatric facilities. As a young girl, you think, he's sick he'll go to the hospital and then he will come home better. However, this hasn't been the case with John. Nothing can stop the voices that he hears in his head. What he hears in his head is similar to when you listen to a radio that is on two channels. He hears a lot of static and voices that do not make any sense. He has called the White House because he thinks that the CIA or FBI put a chip in his head that makes him hear voices. He doesn't know how the voices got there, but he wants to return to his normal state. He wants to return to his state of mind before he took the brown LSD.

I wonder what he could have done with his life. He

was handsome and charismatic. He was a kind and helpful soul. Instead, he sleeps most of his days away. He has to be on antipsychotic drugs that have a lot of side effects and cause him to have severe joint pain. He can't work and no longer has any friends.

I tell you this story about my brother because taking drugs is one of the quickest routes to totaling wrecking your life. When I told friends and acquaintances that I was writing this book, they all wanted to share stories about friends or family members who have totally ruined their lives with drugs. I am sharing this with you because I've only selected three stories regarding how drugs can ruin your life. However, there are thousands of stories out there. Drugs are always a bad choice, no matter how glamorous people make them. They alter your personality on a permanent basis.

Drugs as a Mask

This brings me to another story about a young boy named Joe. Joe is in ninth grade. He thought that it was cool to hang around with the older kids in High School. At first, they didn't want him around because they thought that he would rat on them about their drug use. Over and over again, he watched them use cocaine. As time passed, they let him try cocaine and he became a user himself. Joe told me that he never thought that using cocaine one time would lead him to become an addict and eventually land him in a rehabilitation center during the summer of ninth grade. Using drugs one time led to another and another time until it became a habit.

When Joe told me his story, he was in his junior year. He stated that his life had been hell because of drugs. He told me that one night he stayed up all night drinking with one of his friends. He witnessed his friend take drugs. Later that morning, when he tried to wake up his friend, his friend started convulsing and his eyes were rolling in the back of his head. He tried sticking his fingers down his friend's throat to regurgitate the drugs that were in his system. He also tried pouring cold water on him, but he wouldn't wake up. His friend was overdosing. Feeling panicked, he called the Police. Before the Police arrived, Joe went home, still in shock.

A whole array of feelings were rushing through his head. Was his friend going to live or die? Was he going to get in trouble for being there that night? Would he be charged as an accessory in his friend's death? Could he have prevented his friend's death? As he ran home, he felt afraid, sad, anxious, guilty and full of regret. How could he have played a role in his friend's death?

Although he witnessed this drug overdose in his freshman year, the allure of drugs was too strong for Joe to quit. He started selling drugs to make money in his sophomore year of school. The decision to sell drugs, led him into an even darker place. At a party, he was severely beaten because people knew that he had drugs and money on him. This beating required numerous stitches and nearly took off his ear.

He got caught on school property with marijuana and arrested. At the time of this arrest, he was already on probation. When he was called out of class by the Vice Principal and the Dean of Students, he thought about running. He didn't know how to get out of the situation. He felt a great sense of dread regarding what was about to happen. When he arrived at the office, there was a Police Officer there waiting to arrest him for class D possession.

During this time, he knew how much his behavior had disappointed his mother. She came to the High School and was crying. His father had died of an accidental death years earlier. His mother was the foundation of his life. He loved his mother, but even that love didn't stop him from destroying his own future and hurting her.

As a result of his drug use, in his junior year of high school, Joe was committed to the Department of Youth Services until he was eighteen years old. When he was in the courtroom, he was in shackles and handcuffs. Joe said that the saddest moment of his life was when he turned around and saw his mother sobbing uncontrollably, after the judge committed him to the Department of Youth Services. He knew how much his behavior was hurting his mother and ruining his life. However, he was now addicted to drugs. His addiction was too strong to overcome. Nothing would get in the way of his addiction to the drugs: not his mother, family members or his friends.

He was scared. He was in a holding cell for five hours. His mind was racing because he did not know what lied ahead of him in juvenile services jail. After he was transported to juvenile services, he was fed some disgusting hot dogs and made to shower with strange smelling soap. He didn't talk with anyone. He felt so alone and cried himself to sleep. He had no idea what was coming ahead for him in the detention center. He was miserable and scared. He knew that he would have to watch his back every second of every day. He realized, when it was too late that drugs had hurt his family, himself and robbed him of a lot of time.

Years earlier, when Joe was 5 years old, his father died. His father came home from work and said, "Call 911, something bad is going to happen to me". The ambulance came and took him to the hospital and he later died at the hospital of a heart attack. Years later in counseling, Joe wrote a letter to his father. The letter was written to help him deal with all of his suppressed emotions from years earlier. For some reason, deep down, Joe had blamed himself for his father's death. Joe may have thought that his father's heart attack was because he was playing catch with him. A five year old child's perception of events is totally centered on themselves. No one realized that Joe had buried his feelings and was feeling a deep sense of shame and blame about his father's death. Drugs helped to mask this shame and blame, but in the end things got much worse.

I never heard what happened to the boy who overdosed. I'm not sure if the overdose left his brain impaired in some sort of way. However, I do know of an overdose story that ended in total physical and mental impairment of the person.

My husband works in the field of physical therapy. As part of his job, he sometimes works on the traumatic brain injury floor. One day, he met a twenty eight year old boy. This boy could barely speak. He could not walk and had minimal use of his hands. He wore diapers because he could not control his bladder. He had to live in the nursing home because he could not care for himself. He had all of these physical impairments from overdosing on drugs.

One day he mumbled, "My life is horrible". His life was horrible. When he first started taking drugs, I'm sure that he didn't imagine ending up on a traumatic brain floor of a rehabilitation center. His choice took away his ability to walk, use his arms, speak and even control his bodily fluids. His life would never be the same and it was very, very depressing. You only hear about overdoses that end in death on the news. You don't hear about the thousands of stories of people who end up in nursing homes, also known as a rehabilitation centers because of a drug overdose.

Some people think that it is cool to be in a rehab.

It's not cool to be in a place because your brain can no longer control your bodily functions. What is cool is to control your attitude and your choices, so that you end up having a good life. I am 100% confident that if the boy in the rehabilitation center was able to live his life in reverse and was faced with the choice of whether or not to take drugs, he would not take them. It's too bad that people don't think about the consequences of their choices, when they are faced with making a decision.

Drugs and Suicide

This next story has the worst outcome of all because the boy lost all hope. His mother and father informed him that they were getting a divorce. The news of his mother and father's divorce deeply affected this young man. He especially did not like the fact that his father was already dating again. He started to drink and do drugs, to eradicate the pain.

His family had not realized that he was in pain, when he went off to college. His family had high hopes for him. He was their shining star. He was a handsome, well-rounded Boyscout, an excellent baseball player and a champion swimmer. However, things were about to take a turn for the worst.

When he was twenty- one years old, he impregnated a girl. After she became pregnant, he had a terrible relationship with the baby's mother. It destroyed the relationship, that he had with this girl. This was a constant source of stress in his life. Being a parent, while in college proved to be very difficult for this young man. However, he continued to go to college.

Then one day without warning, the boy's mother received a phone call informing her that her son was dead. He hanged himself. In a New York minute, he was gone and he changed everyone's life, who knew him and loved him. They would never be the same. His death had ripped a piece of their heart away and it would never return.

No one knew that he was in such a dark place. When they went in to his college apartment, they found all types of drug paraphernalia around the room. There was so much paraphernalia that it was easy to deduce that this boy was a drug addict. It all started to make sense. He always needed extra money and was maxing out credit cards to buy food. He had lost his teeth, due to drug use.

His family was absolutely devastated to hear about his death. He was pursuing a college degree to help adolescents. His experience with his parent's divorce could have helped so many children, sometime in the future. However, that bright future was snuffed out, due to his depression from drug use.

His family cried and cried and blamed themselves. When there is a suicide, survivors tend to blame themselves. They questioned why they didn't do more or see more signs. The survivors shouldn't blame themselves. Drugs are the real villain in this story and many other stories too.

This young man's life ended before he got a chance to use his gifts. His gift could have helped so many other children.

Unsuspecting Drug Abusers

This next story differs slightly because the drug abusers didn't actively make a choice to abuse drugs. Their drug was prescribed to them by a physician.

There are a lot of athletes in the United States who have become addicted to drugs unintentionally. They got hurt in their sport and went to the doctor. The doctor prescribes Oxycodone. Oxycodone is a pain killer that is similar to heroin.

The patient becomes addicted to this strong narcotic and then turns to the cheaper street drug, heroin. This situation is becoming an epidemic in the United States. Sports are a big business in the United States. There is pressure on people to become great athletes at a young age. This is causing more injuries which in turn creates more prescriptions to be written.

I know good people who were extremely smart and

great athletes. They became addicts. Their lives were ruined because of one injury and taking a drug that was prescribed to them. They are from good families who are now struggling with all of the problems of drug addiction. I am telling you this story because these athletes do not feel that it was an active choice to become an addict, but it still happened. If you are injured there are other less addicting pain killers. Your choices count!

Don't let your life story become another story of drug addiction and pain. The stories of substance abuse may have slightly different twists and turns, but they have one common denominator. The common denominator is ruined relationships and despair. The drug becomes your personality. You no longer exist.

Bullying and Despair

I work for a school department. One day at school, I was visited by a woman, her daughter, and her nine year old son. The woman was deeply troubled because she recently moved her family to the town and her son was being bullied in his new school. She told me that her son was a well-adjusted student at his previous school and had many friends. She needed to move the family because of financial reasons.

She told me that when her son spoke in front of his new peer group, the fourth grade boys would turn their heads as if to indicate that he didn't exist. They would also accuse him of things that he didn't do and yell at him when the teachers weren't looking.

When speaking with this student, his demeanor was very timid. He didn't turn and face me, when he spoke. His body was turned toward his mother and he kept his head down. He had black and red circles under his eyes and he looked extremely tired. I instantly got the impression that this child was going to take his own life.

The woman asked her daughter and her son to leave the room. Once they were gone, she explained to me that her son's demeanor had done a 180 degree turn about since he came to the school. He had only been there for three weeks. At the end of week two, he came home and sat on her lap and cried for two hours. She told me that he never sat on her lap and she has never seen him cry like that. She held him for two hours and cried with him.

This boy's best friend from his previous town had recently died. The mother told me that her son asked her how long it would take him to get to heaven, if he died right now. He wanted to be with his best friend. This absolutely confirmed my strong feeling that this young boy was suicidal.

This child with so much promise had been demoralized to the point of suicidal thoughts in a period of three weeks. Did these bullies have any empathy for this boy? Was it a game or a way for them to entertain themselves? Did some of them know that it was wrong, but were too weak to stand up to the group?

No matter what the answer is to these questions, the impact on this person is horrible. The impact on this boy's family is horrible. He was the youngest of six kids from a very close family. His siblings watched this vibrant boy crumble in a matter of a few weeks and they didn't know what to do.

We transferred the boy to another school. We worked to get him a peer mentor, so he wouldn't feel all alone. We wanted him to have a fresh start with a different peer group. We integrated him in a natural and respectful way into the new classroom.

It is sad to me that this young boy was treated that way. The bullies and everyone should realize that our words and actions matter. If he bottled his emotions up and did not tell his mother, would he explode at a later point in life? Would he act out his rage in a violent manner? We've seen this scene play out in the news over and over again. Words and actions matter!

Sometimes people go through a hard time and they come out stronger. In this case, I hope that he will take his experience with him and it will help him be a more caring person in the future.

I told the boy about Ellen Degeneres. Early in her career, she was told that she wasn't any good. Hollywood was really mean to her. However, she didn't give up. She touches so many lives with her generosity and kindness. The timing wasn't right for her to shine. If she had given up, so many lives wouldn't have been helped. This boy couldn't give up. It's a dark time in his young life that can teach him some valuable life lessons.

But, adults must help him to fix the problem. What would have happened if this boy didn't tell his mother? What would have happened if adults in the school didn't take the necessary steps to correct the problem? This boy's bright light would be snuffed out before he was ever given a chance to shine.

If you see something that isn't right, take the steps to help. You may totally change the direction of that person's life without realizing the huge impact you may have. Who knows? Maybe one kind act could have prevented the shootings in Columbine or Newtown, Connecticut.

If you have a problem, tell someone who you trust about it. Others may have great ideas about how to solve your problem. Everyone in this world has their own unique perspective on things. The other person may have a creative solution to your problem that you never dreamed existed.

Pregnancy

Would you make a choice that limits your mobility, your money, or your freedom without really thinking about it? Of course you wouldn't. Well, that's what you do, when you have sex without thinking about the consequences.

17 girls from Gloucester, Massachusetts allegedly made a pregnancy pact. The alleged pact was that they would all agree to get pregnant at the same time, so that they could raise their babies together. The girls involved with the pact probably wanted someone to love them unconditionally.

What these girls didn't understand is that raising a baby is very expensive. One of the fathers was a 24 year old homeless man. This homeless man could not provide child support or emotional support. Because these girls chose to get pregnant, their life had drastically changed. Going forward, their choices were extremely limited. Now it was more difficult for them to travel, go to college, exercise, try different occupations, go on dates, and hang out with their friends. Whatever they wanted to do, took extra planning and/or money for a babysitter. Their life was no longer care free. They were constantly tired from lack of sleep and they were instantly an adult with bills and responsibilities.

When faced with pregnancy, some individuals try to take the so called easy way out and have an abortion. I have known individuals who have chosen to have an abortion instead of keeping the baby or putting the baby up for adoption. They see this as the easiest way for them.

It's funny how life is full of karma. Even though at the time, this was the easiest option for her, life had a funny way of repaying her. Due to this abortion, the lining of her uterus was scarred. Years later, she met a new boy and was deeply in love with him. They got married and were expecting a baby. Due to her previous abortion and scarring, her uterus burst, while she was having the baby. The baby was in a pool of blood and almost died. If the baby wasn't saved in time, the baby could have had brain damage that would have led to a lifetime of around the clock care by the mother. Her new baby could have been in a wheelchair, on a ventilator, need physical therapy, occupational therapy and nursing care. Luckily for her, she was at the hospital, when her uterus burst. Therefore, both mother and baby were saved.

I'm sure that her previous abortion crossed her mind. If she hadn't had that abortion, would this have happened? If she hadn't had an abortion, how old would the child be now? Would the two children look alike? In this moment that should be the happiest moment of her life, deep regret kicked in. How could one decision to have sex years ago have such an impact on her again today, over fifteen years later?

The doctors told her and her husband not to have any more children because it could risk her life. Since the first born baby was a female, her husband wanted to have a boy. They did eventually have a boy, but it resulted in the wife feeling bitter toward her husband. She felt that he did not care about her life, he only wanted a son. This bitterness festered until they eventually divorced. If she could live her life in reverse, I'm sure that she would have chosen not to have sex that night. Not having sex would have been the easiest road. Instead regret, divorce and bitterness were the byproduct of a bad decision. Now, her days are spent battling with her ex-husband and trying to pay for her children on one income. Bitterness and poverty were not what she dreamed for her life at a younger age. However, her choices lead her to a place that she did not like.

Parenting

My friend's daughter met a handsome boy from New York. They quickly became very close. She became pregnant and they decided to keep the baby. The boy moved in with the girl's family. When the girl was approximately five months pregnant, the family received word from New York, that this boy was a sex offender and was wanted in New York as a criminal.

They quickly kicked him out of the house. However, prior to his departure, the Police Department sent out flyers to everyone in the neighborhood informing the neighbors of the level 3 sex offender located at their address. This was very humiliating for this girl and her family. This girl was left alone and pregnant with a sex offender's baby. That one decision forever changed her life! I'm sure if she could do it over again, the story would have a different outcome. She would much rather be out on the dating scene and meet someone nice. However, she is left with a constant reminder when she looks into her baby's eyes of this brief period of time that changed her life forever.

If these girls weren't feeling loved, they should use positive techniques to increase their confidence and self-worth. Instead they dug themselves into a hole of loneliness and self-despair.

I asked someone who I knew if I could tell her story. Her story is similar to the stories above. She became pregnant and has been struggling ever since. She did not want me to tell the details of her story because she feels that it will not help people. She said, "People have to make their own mistakes". I started to really analyze her words. Is this true? Do people have to make their own mistakes or can they learn from others? I've come to the conclusion that people can learn from others. They can learn if they pay attention to the errors of others and they don't repeat them in their lives. The reason why people make mistakes is because they don't think about the outcome of their choices.

Drugs and pregnancy are two quick ways to alter your life forever. If we lived our life in reverse and we knew that we were going to end up in jail for doing drugs or we would carry a sex offender's baby, do you think we'd make the same choices. Of course not! People just don't think about how their choices can affect the rest of their life.

You are the person who is in the driver's seat of your life. Be an active driver. Don't let autopilot take over your life and drive you down a dark road. You are meant to feel joy and pain in your life. When you feel pain, don't mask it with drugs or alcohol. The pain you feel won't be forever. It will more than likely teach you something, in the end, if you pay attention. You might not know what the lesson is right away, but it will eventually come to you.

Like Mariah Carey says, "The hero lies in you". You have the opportunity to drive yourself to a great spot. Take advantage of your opportunities.

Can of Worms

Life can be funny. Sometimes doing the wrong thing can open up a whole can of worms. Even if you think the law or rule is silly, by not obeying it, you open the door of negativity for yourself. For example, there was a young man who wanted to make a few extra dollars scalping baseball tickets. However, one fateful day, a Police Officer spotted him. A foot chase ensued. The scalper thought he got away because he managed to jump into a cab. The Police Officer caught up with the cab because it got stuck in traffic.

By this time, the Police Officer was infuriated and started to viciously grab the scalper. The scalper fought back and was pushing and hitting the officer. The scalper was charged with scalping tickets, but also received a much worse charge of assault and battery on a Police Officer.

Later on in his life, this scalper decided that he wanted to work with children. He realized that working with children is his passion. Unfortunately, employers don't want employees working around children who have assault and battery charges on their record. He never guessed that scalping tickets to a baseball game would have such a long lasting effect on his life. Opening the door and doing one thing illegally, led to a much more serious charge. He wishes for a do-over for that day, I'm sure. Because he didn't thoroughly weigh his decision to scalp tickets that day, he forfeited his passion later in life; his passion to work with children.

Choices

How do we make sure that we make the right choices for our life? Well, for starters, you should think about your choices, when they are in front of you. Don't allow your life to be on autopilot. Autopilot may not take you where you wish to go. You have control over your own decisions, so you should exercise your control. There are so many things that are out of your control in life. Why would you give up the control that you have; your decisions.

We tend to think that we are supposed to be happy all of the time. It would be nice if we were happy all of the time, but it's not realistic. There are a lot of bad things that happen in the world today. We are supposed to feel joy, sadness, anger, anxiety, boredom and pain. These feelings are all meant to tell us something.

However, in today's society, we don't sit still enough to really listen to ourselves. We mask our feelings with overloaded schedules, sex, gambling, food, alcohol and drugs. Denying our emotions is a well-known cause of addictions. These types of addictions can make your life spiral out of control. We often don't even realize that we are in a downward spiral because we are still trying to mask the bad thing that happened to us months ago.

Instead of creating our own mess, we should understand that these emotions are meant to be part of who we are. We need to be still long enough to work through the feelings. Instead of doing things that are detrimental to us, we should write down our feelings or talk them over with a friend or family member. We can also just sit quietly to think through our sadness. Many people exercise away stress and sadness. Allow yourself the time to grieve through whatever problem you have. I can't stress this enough. Learn to be still. Sit quietly, relax, think about everything and live your emotions. Live your emotions!

When someone dies, I often hear people say that it will take a year for the grieving person to get over it. This is ridiculous to me. How can someone tell another person how long their emotions will last? Similarly, it takes patients different amounts of time to heal from their medical trauma; it takes people various amounts of time to heal from emotional trauma.

When I was younger, prior to a large rain storm, I would feel pain in my knees. I told an adult that I thought I had arthritis. The person told me that I was too young for arthritis and that it couldn't be true. Now that I'm older, I still have the same pains before it rains, but now they believe me that it is arthritis. My point is that people can be foolish and they will try to talk you out of your own feelings. You know yourself better than anyone and don't second guess your feelings.

Middle school and high school is a demanding time on the emotions of a person. You want to fit in and there is a lot of pressure to conform in various ways. This period of time, approximately four to five years can have a major impact on your later life.

How can you ever have any respect for yourself, if concede to what the group wants every time? By giving in, you knock yourself down a peg in the game of self-respect. Your self-respect and confidence will follow you wherever you go, for years to come.

Early on, we build habits. No one in your life will be with you every step of the way. You will meet all sorts of people, good and bad. If you don't care about yourself and you don't stand up for yourself, you are starting a bad habit. You don't have to be mean or aggressive, when standing up for yourself. You can get your point across without yelling.

If someone offers you drugs and you decline, they may say something mean. What would you rather, a few minutes of mean comments or a life time of addiction, stealing to get drug money, rotted teeth, hurting your loved ones and in and out rehabilitation centers, and cold sweats. People think, "yah right" that won't happen, if I smoke pot.

Things don't happen right away, but they have a way of opening up a negative door. You may not want to see what's at the end of the hallway, once you've taken that door. Take my story about the ticket scalper. It seemed like a quick way to make a few extra dollars, right? I'm sure that the scalper never dreamed that when he set out to make a few extra dollars, he'd end up with a criminal record of assaulting a police officer. Scalping opened up a negative door for this man; that he's been trying to close for years.

Sometimes we look at life and think it is unfair. Your best friend is better looking, better at sports or has more money. It's human nature to compare ourselves. However, when you do, realize that no one's life is perfect. In High School, I had a friend, who had it all. She was beautiful and modeled. She was from an extremely affluent family. They had vacation houses everywhere. She had a lot of friends and a great sense of humor. Her mother and father were both very nice and very attractive too. You get the picture. She had it going on.

However, later on in our lives, she admitted to me

that although, on the surface, everything was great, her family lived in turmoil. Her father worked a lot and her mother would get angry. This created a lot of yelling in the family home and a lot of tension. However, the public persona was to never let it show. Sometimes when we are living a lie, no matter how big or how small, it creates tension in ourselves. Burying the truth is a quick way to addiction and other emotional issues.

So, the next time you are jealous of someone, think of their life like a ruler. You may only see one inch of that person's life right now. You're seeing the perfect part. What about the other eleven inches of their life. As I got older and viewed my friend's entire life, this analogy became very clear to me. No one gets away with a perfect life!

The ruler analogy can be applied to your life too. You may be in the bad part of your life. This inch of your ruler is terrible. Everyone goes through bad periods; it's natural. However, your choices and how you deal with the bad period can impact the remaining portion of your life.

Sometimes the bad things that happen to us are meant to set us on a different path; a path to much better things.

Letting go of the past in order to move on

Have you ever known someone who had something bad happen to them, but they can't let go. They may talk about it all of the time. This person may feel like they are always the victim or a martyr. They may feel that they have terrible luck or that people are out to get them. These type of people need to let go of the past, so that they can move forward and grow. If you recognize yourself as one of these people, you need to let go. If you don't let go, you will stay stuck in a negative pattern.

I know someone in this sort of negative pattern. The negativity started around forty years ago and it still living alive and well right now because the person will not let go. In essence, they are contaminating those around them because they won't let go.

This person grew up feeling that that her mother hated her. She thought her mother liked her other siblings, but did not like her. On the outside, she lived a relatively normal life. She got married and had children. However, the drama continued.

Over the months and years, I watched this person have all sorts of fights with her children. There was so much turmoil in the family: suicide, money issues, unwanted pregnancies, constant sibling fighting and always blaming someone else for issues. It doesn't take a rocket scientist to see that there are family problems stemming from the negativity of the mother. Everyone is an enemy.

What type of person do you want as a friend, coworker or neighbor? Do you want someone who always has some type of negative drama or would you want a person who takes accountability for their own actions?

I'm not denying that these types of people had something bad happen to them. But since they cannot put it behind them, they perpetuate the negativity. They can't live in a good state of mind. They deserve a state of mind that is free from negativity, revenge and anger. Logically, if someone told them that they would carry a grudge from 11 years old until they were fifty and basically infect everyone around them, they wouldn't choose to do that.

However, by not letting go, that is exactly what they

are doing. Maybe they were told by someone to "get over it" at a young age. Maybe they didn't allow themselves to grieve through whatever happened to them early on. Living their feelings and grieving at an early age would have allowed them to move on. We all get hurt. Life is not perfect. Move past the hurt. Move to the positive and live the life that you deserve.

This person would have had a much better life, if she grieved through her pain at a younger age and got over it. Instead she affected the rest of her life. She allowed one inch of her life's ruler to take over the other eleven inches.

Controlling Anxiety

We all have a pessimistic voice inside us at times. You know the voice, "You're going to miss the basketball hoop" or "You're not going to present well in front of the class". You want to take control away from this inner voice and take back control of your life. Dan Jones an author of 'Take Control of Your Life' states that you should give this inner voice a really boring, monotone voice. This helps your inner voice from having power to control your destiny. It puts the voice in its' place.

Anxiety or the pessimistic inner voice can prevent you from doing things that you're meant to do. It prevents you from being a star. If babies had this inner pessimistic voice, they would never learn to walk. Their inner voice would say, "You can't do it". "You keep falling down". "You just fell 5 times and stumble 5 times". "Forget it!"

Every entrepreneur knows that mistakes are vital to success. They learn from their mistakes and they keep getting better. They don't let their inner voice say, "What a big mistake –you're a failure" "Forget it". They learn and become the shining star that they are meant to be. Great scientists build their science experiments off of this philosophy. They test things out and learn from their failures.

Inspirations of Perseverance and Challenge

As stated by Henry Ford, "Failure is the opportunity to begin again, more intelligently". We all make mistakes. This is your chance to learn from your mistakes and move on. Begin the next inch of your ruler, striving for your goals. Our goals always take longer than the time that we anticipate. Perseverance is the key to success in life.

There was an Olympic skater, whose sister was dying of cancer. He promised her that he would win her an Olympic medal. He probably thought that if he worked really hard and won an Olympic medal, she could work really hard and beat cancer. He skated and did not win a medal. All of his hours and hours of preparation didn't matter. He was devastated. His sister passed away from cancer. He felt deep, deep despair. He did not live up to his promise. How could he do that to his sister? Now, his sister was gone.

However, he did not give up and his life continued on. He continued to practice and practice. He had a daughter and named her after his sister. Five years later, he won the Olympic medal, except this time, it was even sweeter. In the victory circle, he skated with his daughter, named after his sister, in his arms. There is no doubt in my mind that his thoughts were on his sister. Day in and day out practicing couldn't have been easy, but his perseverance paid off and made the victory that much sweeter.

Confucius said, "The greater the obstacle, the more the glory in overcoming it". Whatever the obstacle is in your life, work toward overcoming it. Many extremely successful people have had huge obstacles to overcome. Look at Oprah Winfrey. She had a rough childhood. However, she liked to read. By reading, she realized that there is more to life than what she was seeing in her home. As a young child, she had many obstacles. Although she makes it look easy, I'm sure that she had many obstacles along the way too. No one can escape these things that happen to us. It's how we deal with the good and bad, that determines who we are.

When you are in your teen years, your brain is still developing. You live for excitement. That is why gossip is so prevalent during the teen years. It's an irony in life that the part of your brain that you need the most during your teen years, is still in its infancy stage. The part of your brain that I'm referring to is your frontal lobe. Your frontal lobe controls judgment and impulse control skills.

Therefore, you need to be extra careful to think about your decisions, before you act or react. When cutting wood, carpenters use a technique ensuring that they don't make a mistake. They measure the wood twice and cut it once. This helps the carpenter avoid a lot of wasted wood. Teenagers should use this same philosophy; think twice, act once. Think twice, act once.

By using this simple technique, you may avoid a life altering decision. Don't end up with regret in your life.

Some people have a rocky start to their lives. Maybe their parents are addicted to drugs, neglect them or are extremely hurtful with their words. When you're young, this may affect your self-confidence. You may have shame, embarrassment or even disgust for your family.

Again, looking at the ruler, this period in your life may be 1-2 inches of the ruler. Similar to Oprah, you may want to consider reading to barricade yourself from the negativity. You may think of a more creative, positive way to barricade yourself. Find your way, so that you don't turn to drugs, alcohol or other destructive mechanisms. This period of your life is tough, but it doesn't have to be forever. Forever is based on your decisions and how you deal with the here and now.

I am hopeful that after you read this book, you will stop and really think about your choices. Stop, think twice and act once will always help you, no matter how old you are.

What happens if you feel that you don't have control over the choices you make? Maybe your parent is an alcoholic or drug addict, your parents are divorced, or you were a foster child shipped from household to household. Day to day is a struggle and your self-esteem has suffered from the adults around you.

Sometimes when there is trouble in a family, the children can feel at fault or bad about themselves. Understand that this is not your fault. You should build yourself a wall of resiliency. In studying resiliency, I've found that people who are resilient understand that everything is not their fault and they find ways to feel good about themselves.

This is where the real challenge for you comes into play. You don't have to play the victim. Find someone whom you can confide in. It may be a teacher, a neighbor, or the parents of a good friend. If you have the attitude that this is a challenge instead of having a defeatist attitude, it will help you move to a better life.

Some of the great performers used hard times to drive them into success. Al Pacino, the lead actor in the Godfather was asked where his rage comes from when he acts. Movie critics state that his rage seems so real. Some people feel that Al Pacino has been able to isolate his earlier feelings of injustice and anger and channel it into a wonderful acting career. He was raised by a single mother in the Bronx. He was a High School dropout. He slept on the streets of Greenwich Village and before he made it big in acting. He had no money and no food at times. During this time, he met a man named Charlie Laughton, who became his mentor and his friend. Al Pacino could have easily given up. However, his perseverance and finding the right mentor paid off for him.

When he obtained the role in the Godfather, no one wanted him in this role except Francis Ford Coppola. Even as they were shooting, Coppola too was questioning his judgment about whether Pacino was right. He seemed too passive to be a mobster.

However, what they didn't know is that Pacino had studied the script and he was purposefully acting passive in the beginning to show the transition in the young boy's life as he became more involved with the mob. It was brilliant and earned him an academy award. He was an instant star.

I bring up the story about Al Pacino because resilient people don't let adversary define them. Al Pacino could have thought to himself that he had to steal, due to a lack of money. However, he was resilient. Resilient people find a mentor and set goals for themselves. They reach their goals and move beyond them. This helps them out of their current circumstance on to something better. Resilient people can see that they can have a different kind of life. They understand that their current situation does not have to be permanent.

Another resilient individual is magician, David Blaine. David too was raised by a single mother in New York. He did not have a privileged upbringing. He stated, "When I'm most alive is when I'm challenging myself". Challenging yourself to move beyond your current situation builds resilience.

I personally believe that the reason why people who win the lottery are so miserable is because they no longer strive for anything. Many children who are raised in affluent families and given everything, no longer strive for anything. Warren Beatty, one the richest men in America didn't give his children everything. They had chores and goals. Everything wasn't handed to them. So, the next time you have to work really hard for something that you want, remember that deep down, humans need this sort of goal.

Forgiveness

Can you ever forgive the horrible things that someone has done to you? Sometimes forgiveness takes time. We all want everything resolved right away. Our life and emotions happen in stages. Forgiveness and trust do not necessarily have to go hand in hand. You can forgive someone but still use caution about whether to trust them. The best case scenario would be if you could have forgiveness and trust. However, many times life is more complicated than that.

Forgiveness is the best gift that you can give yourself. Like Nelson Mandella said, "not forgiving is like drinking a cup of poison every day and hoping that it kills your enemy".

Years ago, a girl who was three years old was sitting on her stairs in Boston. She was hit by a stray bullet in a gang rivalry. She instantly became paralyzed from the waist down. I too had a child who was three years old at that time. I was so grief stricken by this story, that I wrote the mother and child a letter.

In the letter I told that mother how beautiful her daughter was and that I hoped that she didn't let this negative thing take away her daughter's special spirit that I could see in her. Later on that year, the news did a story about the mother and her paralyzed daughter.

The story was about how this mother and daughter forgave the gang member. Their forgiveness changed the gang member's life. Although he was in prison for his crime, their forgiveness was the conduit that turned the prisoner's life around. He vowed to help others.

Now, seven years later the news did another story about this family. The young girl is now ten years old. She is still paralyzed from the waist down. However, her mother's truly loving spirit has rubbed off on her daughter. The young girl realizes the importance of forgiveness. She is much wiser than a regular ten year old girl. In the news story, the girl talks about how to relieve angry feelings. She tells people to take a walk or do something nice for yourself, when you're feeling angry. This will help you to feel less stressed and you're less apt to take out your negative feelings on someone else. The mother said, "Hurt people go on to hurt others". This statement is so true!

If you're hurt and you're having trouble forgiving, don't drink the cup of poison. Do something that you enjoy to take away your angry feelings. Don't go on to hurt others. If everyone stopped the negativity within themselves, instead of passing along hurt feelings, the world would be a better place. My personal opinion is that many bullies are feeling hurt themselves and they pass that hurt onto others. Take the higher ground. Be the shock absorber that stops the hate.

Like Stevie Wonder says in his song, "I'm gonna keep on trying until I reach the highest ground. No one is gonna burn me down. Let nobody burn you down."

Don't let anyone stop you from being what you're meant to be. Anger and bitterness can prevent you from being your best. Be aware of this. Don't be on autopilot.

The story of Tyler Perry really opened my eyes to forgiveness versus trust. Tyler Perry was beaten by his father. He has forgiven his father, so that he can remain positive in life. However, he chooses not to see his father. He pays for his father's house out of respect for his father's role as parent. In listening to Tyler's story, it appears that he has forgiven his father, but he uses caution in his relationship with his father. Self-preservation is not a mean thing. Tyler Perry does a lot of good. If he did not take care of himself, he would not be capable of doing all of the good deeds that he does for others. Remember, be true to yourself!

Sometimes adversity can bring us together instead of apart. Our reaction to adversity and how we show forgiveness can alter someone's life forever. One of the most touching expressions of forgiveness, that I saw first-hand is the story of Matt Brown. Matt was a Norwood High School hockey player. During a game with Weymouth, Massachusetts, Matt was checked into the boards. He went down and was not moving. In a typical manner, everyone held their breath and was waiting for him to get up. But he never did get up. He was taken out of the ice arena on a stretcher. Later on that evening, we learned that he was paralyzed from the chest down. We were all horrified.

How could life change so drastically for Matt and his family in the blink of an eye? His family was well known in the community for their good deeds. His grandfather was a well-known pediatrician who helped numerous kids become better. This time he couldn't even help his own grandson. His grandmother has a baseball field named after her for her commitment to sports in the town. His mother, father, aunts and uncles are the best type of people you can meet. Warm, caring, and involved. They constantly help others.

Right from the start the community rallied around Matt Brown and his family. There were numerous fundraisers to help them with medical bills. A big gala was held at Patriot Plaza, donated by Bob Kraft, the owner of the Patriots. Local carpenters helped to renovate the Brown family home, so that it was compatible for a wheelchair. Matt spent many days, weeks and months in a rehabilitation hospital. When he finally arrived home at the Norwood airport, he was greeted by all of his friends and family members. He was the same smiling Matt Brown.

Now let's fast forward a year. Although still paralyzed, Matt remains on the hockey team and attends the games. When he graduated high school, they retired his number. On the one year anniversary of becoming paralyzed, coincidentally, Norwood High School was playing Weymouth High School again. Traditionally, Norwood High hockey parents hold a spaghetti dinner on Friday nights, prior to their home games on Saturday nights. The Brown family volunteered to hold the dinner on the one anniversary of Matt becoming paralyzed.

Typically these dinners were only for Norwood parents and players. The Brown family rented out a restaurant and extended their hand to the parents and players of Weymouth. They brought both teams together to bridge this terrible thing that happened one year earlier.

They didn't want the Weymouth team to feel shameful about what happened. The Browns made shirts and hats with Mattie's number on them for the Weymouth and Norwood parents to wear during the game. The Weymouth and Norwood parents and players all ate together and got to know one another. At the game that Saturday night, they were all wearing Mattie's number.

If the Brown family did not extend their forgiveness in this manner, the hockey player who checked Matt may have secretly felt shame and disgrace, for the rest of his life. Right after Matt was checked and it was clear that he was paralyzed from the chest down, the Browns went to the media to state that it was not the Weymouth player's fault. They stated that it was a freak accident. If the Brown family harbored anger or bitterness toward the other hockey player instead of public forgiveness, it could have had a severe impact on the hockey player's conscience and potentially affected him for the rest of his life.

You may think that high school boys would forget about their friend. He can no longer walk. He can't play sports, go bowling, chase after girls, go to the movies and all sorts of other things that boys do in high school. His friends didn't care. They stand by him. Matt's father allows his friends to drive the handicap accessible van. They take him out to socialize and they help him with his medical needs while they are out.

There are no grudges. There is forgiveness. There is reaching out a hand in an act of kindness and there is never forgetting your friend. Matt's family and friends are truly wonderful role models for Matt. Without their guidance of forgiveness and friendship, it would have been more difficult for Matt to forgive. The forgiveness in this story should be shown more often in our society. We all have the choice to forgive. Forgiveness is a wonder prompter of peace and togetherness. It transforms lives!

Balance

As I get older, I realize that life has a way of balancing itself out for most people. Those who had a bad childhood have good fortune later in life. Oprah and Tyler Perry are two examples of bad situations turned good. At high school reunions all over the country, it is ironic to see this balance played out. The mean girls are still mean, living a sad, shallow life. The unpopular high school students who were bullied become very successful. They are the doctors and lawyers in the group. How rewarding it is to see this sense of balance happen for people.

Those who had everything early on, have unfortunate occurrences later in life. Once such example of this is regarding a boy with whom I went to High School. He was handsome, always had a very attractive girlfriend. He was very intelligent and very athletic. He graduated High School and went to Harvard University. From every account, he had everything, intelligence, looks and athleticism.

However, somewhere down the road things soured. He began to gamble, drink and do drugs. Because of his reckless behavior, he lost his job and his wife. Then, many years after high school, he tried to take his own life by jumping in front of a bus. How sad, that this person who had it all, now had lost all hope and tried to take his own life.

Life has its ups and downs. That is how we learn and grow. If we look at the ups and downs of life this way, through an optimistic lens, we endure much better in life. The negative parts of our life have just as much to teach us as the positive parts of our life. Unfortunately, this young man turned to addictions during the down portion of his life. This created a downward spiral that he couldn't stop. Hopelessness and despair took over.

That is what inspired me to write this book. I started to realize that so many people ruin their lives by not making conscious decisions.

One Special You

Don't let negative people around you affect your self-esteem. I have a family member who is extremely selfish and manipulative. For years, this person has manipulated and has been extremely hurtful to my family.

For years, I've tried to be nice to this person. Then one day, I grew up. I realized that no matter what I do, I can't change her. I somehow associated her terrible behavior and abusive personality with my families' identity. As stated earlier, young people have a very self-centered view of the world. Now, I realize that her actions have nothing to do with me or my family. She made her own choices.

If you were born into a certain type of family and it is making you feel discouraged, remember the ruler. You can build the remaining part of your life's ruler to be much better. Negative individuals are everywhere in life. Sometimes they are our family members, sometimes they are our supervisors and sometimes they are our friends. Don't get caught up in the craziness that surrounds them. That's what they do best. They will draw you into all sorts of drama. It will zap your energy and potentially your self-worth.

Conserve your energy for things that will help you. It is a tip that I learned later in my life, so I want you to know early on.

Negative words and actions really hurt. There are countless stories of individuals who cut their life short by believing what others say about them instead of living up to their potential in life. They are cutting short their gifts. How sad it is when people waste the gifts that have been given to them. Look at Ellen DeGeneres. Early on, she was ostracized from Hollywood because she openly announced that she was gay. She didn't give up. With patience and perseverance, she continued on and is now one of the top talk shows hosts. Her sense of humor and acceptance of all types of people appeals to a diverse audience. Ellen has helped so many individuals who are less fortunate. She gives them cars, money and most importantly, hope. If Ellen had given up, she would not have been able to help all of those less fortunate people that she helps day in and day out on her show.

Sometimes we are not aware of our gifts because they are yet to surface. Patience and perseverance serves you well in this life. Without both, you will not live to your full potential.

Don't let your brain talk you out of the Impossible

There is a golf professional named Dennis Walters. In 1974, Dennis was in an accident that left him paralyzed from the waist down. Dennis' lifelong dream was to play golf on the PGA tour. His future in golf was looking extremely dim.

Now that he was paralyzed, there were a lot of things that Dennis could no longer do. However, he wasn't willing to give up his love for the game of golf. He started hitting golf balls from his wheelchair and then he progressed to a swivel seat.

He is the host of the Dennis Walters Golf Show. This show is about "Golf Lessons and Life Lessons". A famous quote from Dennis is, "if you have a dream and it doesn't work out, never stop dreaming ... get a new dream!" In his show, he challenges audience members to try something in life that they think is impossible.

He preaches that with hard work and perseverance you can succeed at anything. Don't let your own brain talk you out of trying. Try the impossible! Dennis Walters now has a successful talk show doing 90-100 shows per year. He could have spent those years feeling sorry for himself. Instead, he got out there and achieved the impossible and along the way helped countless people.

Take Aways

I wrote this book to help you realize that you should take control of your decisions early on in your life. Don't let your life go on autopilot. Experience your emotions, good and bad. They are there for a reason. Don't mask your emotions with drugs and alcohol or other addictive or destructive behavior. It takes people various amounts of time to heal from emotional trauma. Allow yourself the time to grieve through whatever problem you have.

If people around you are destructive and hurtful, don't take on their negativity. Do what you can to disassociate with them. This will help you to be more positive and forgiving. Lead your life; don't let it lead you. Remember your life as a ruler. Not all parts will be good or bad. You have many gifts. Don't destroy them before you have the opportunity to use them. In a New York minute, it can all change!

Resilient people don't let adversary define them. Resilient people find a mentor, set goals for themselves and move beyond their current situation. "Failure is the opportunity to begin again, more intelligently". Learn from your mistakes and move on. Begin the next inch of your ruler, striving for your goals. Perseverance is the key to achieving your goals and success in life.

When making decisions, don't forget to stop, think twice and act once. Forgiveness and love are the keys to living a peaceful life.

Remember in the end, the hero lies in you!